# ANI AFSHAR

# BEADED FANTASIES
## Beads & Strings Jewelry

## A Step-by-Step Workshop

Photography by
Jeffrey B. Snyder

4880 Lower Valley Road   Atglen, Pennsylvania  19310

# Foreword

Integrity is the word that comes to mind when I think of the work of ANI AFSHAR. I've met and worked with many, many artists, and designers over the years – rarely have I come across someone with such clear and focused design intention.

Using bead, wire, fiber, and ribbon, Ani creates a very special vocabulary of texture and volume. The reductive silhouettes that she creates often belie the intricate and precise nature of her technique. As a designer myself, I am in awe of the hand agility required in this medium. Ani is the master.

The craft of weaving and bead manipulation is an ancient one. Ani employs this sense of history and, at the same time, succeeds in creating a very contemporary sensibility. Make no mistake - Ani Afshar is a modernist.

I feel honored to have ANI AFSHAR'S work as part of the selection at my business.

**—Gregory Reeves**

In May of 2006, Gregory Reeves opened a retail boutique in the heart of the Greenwich Village neighborhood of New York City – *christopher19design collective*.

Published by Schiffer Publishing Ltd.
4880 Lower Valley Road
Atglen, PA 19310
Phone: (610) 593-1777; Fax: (610) 593-2002
E-mail: Info@schifferbooks.com

For the largest selection of fine reference books on this and related subjects, please visit our web site at **www.schifferbooks.com**
We are always looking for people to write books on new and related subjects. If you have an idea for a book please contact us at the above address.

This book may be purchased from the publisher.
Include $3.95 for shipping.
Please try your bookstore first.
You may write for a free catalog.

In Europe, Schiffer books are distributed by
Bushwood Books
6 Marksbury Ave.
Kew Gardens
Surrey TW9 4JF England
Phone: 44 (0) 20 8392-8585; Fax: 44 (0) 20 8392-9876
E-mail: info@bushwoodbooks.co.uk
Website: www.bushwoodbooks.co.uk

# Contents

# 10-strand Seed Bead Necklace

This is a 10-strand seed bead necklace with clusters of various beads. We use 6 lb. fine fishing line and 26 guage wire, as needed.

Here is the color palette of beads for the 10-strand necklace.

We begin by making the drops for the clusters of this necklace. There will be ten strands, therefore 10 sets of drops. Use any chain with rings wide enough to fit the wire. Place the chain, the beads, and the seed bead on the wire, like so.

Fold the end of the wire around the seed bead.

Pull the wire back through the large bead and the chain until the seed bead is nestled tightly close to the large bead.

Make a loop around the chain with the round-nose pliers.

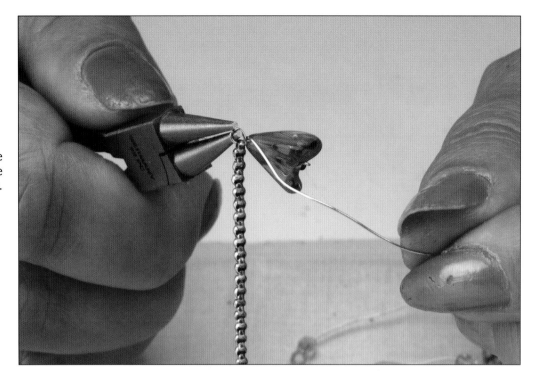

Cut the excess wire off.

Count back six links on the chain and cut.

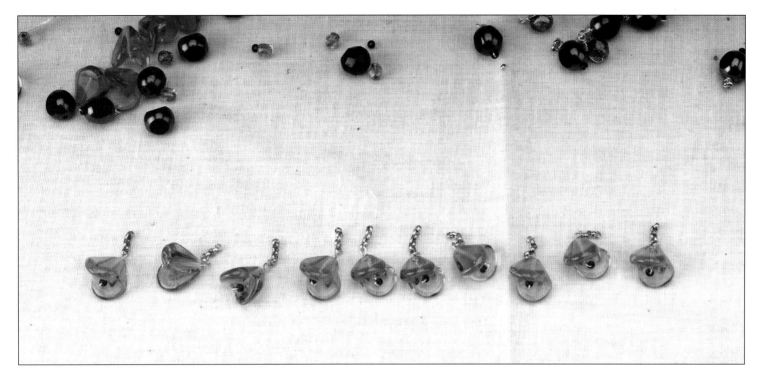

The finished drop. Repeat this until you have ten of these.

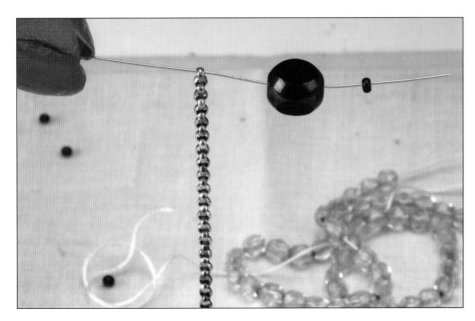

Repeat the same with these 10 beads.

Again, make the loop to secure the chain.

Cut the chain at two links
for this drop.

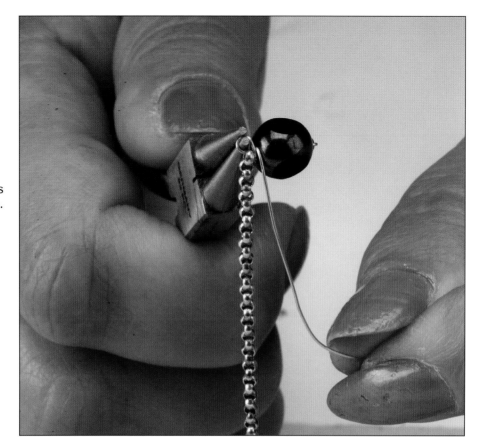

Repeat until you have ten of these as well.

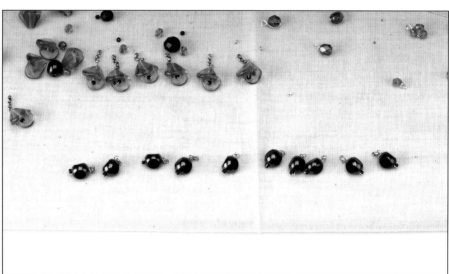

10 finished single drops.

Put three 4 mm. beads on the wire to make a 3-bead drop.

Fold the wire over.

Twist the wire.

Make a loop with the round-nose pliers and wrap the wires tightly around the base of the loop.

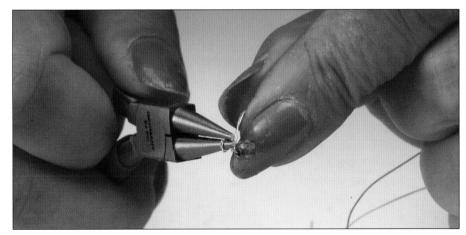

Cut off the excess wires. Here are three completed sets of three bead drops.
You are going to need ten of these as well.
Now make ten one bead drops with 6 mm. beads, following the same steps.

Create your loop and twist the wire around the base to secure.

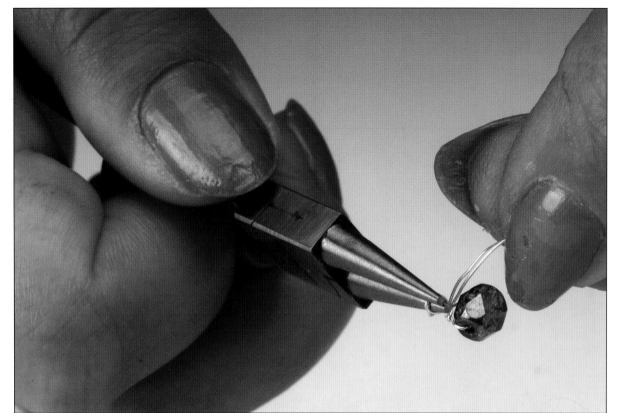

Cut off the excess wire.

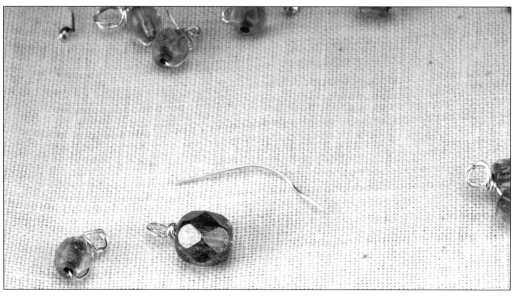

Repeat the steps for the one bead drop with these faceted beads as well.

You can make the necklace any size. This one is 14-inches long. On a hard surface, such as a jewelry tray or fabric-covered foam board (not a pillow), pin two large pins 14 inches apart. The 6 lb. fishing line has to be measured and cut before starting the beading. For 10 strands, measure 14 inches 13 times, and cut once.

Thread your string on a fine beading needle.

Tie a knot in the other end of the wire, making a loop.

Position the drops evenly prior to beading in the 14" space between the two pins.

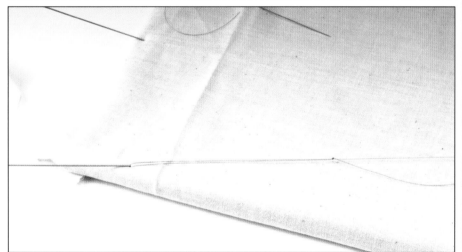

Secure the looped end of your string on the board with a third pin.

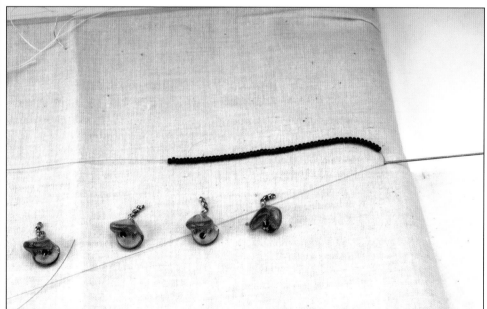

Start stringing the seed beads on your string with the beading needle. Notice the string is now secured at either end with a pin and we will be wrapping the ten strands around these two pins as we go.

When ready for the drops, string a 4mm faceted bead. Place one of each drop on the needle and pull the drops on the thread.

Run the needle back through the 4mm facetted bead, which precedes the drops.

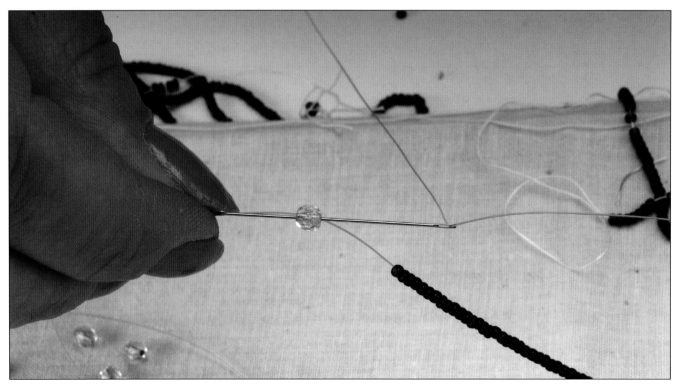

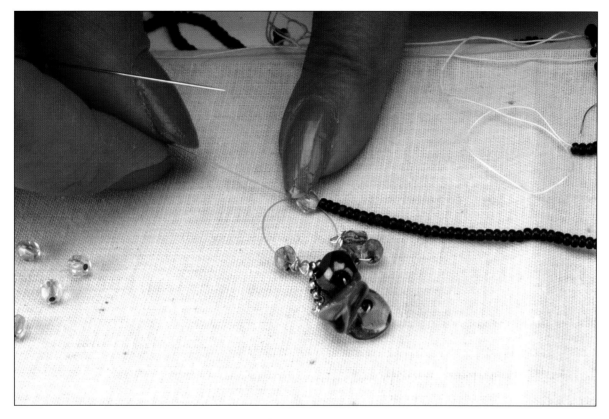

Pull it tight, drawing the drops up against the faceted bead.

Like this.

Add more seed beads and every now and then place a larger bead as well. Keep the thread loose so it does not tangle as you go.

Loop the thread back around the pin, maintaining the 14" necklace size, and keep beading. We're going to do this ten times.

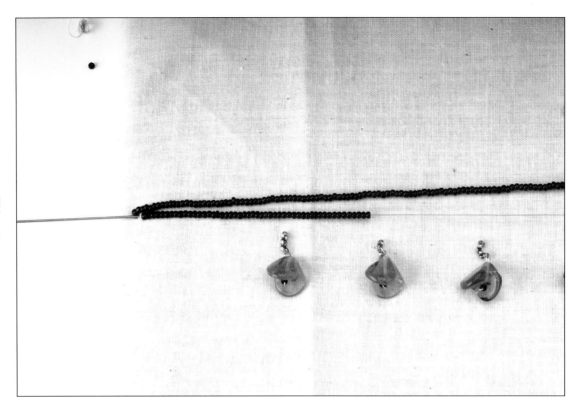

Now bead the second cluster, using the same method as before. Place the faceted bead first, followed by the drops. Notice that the clusters should be spaced in different places, one cluster per strand spread out evenly on the necklace.

Run the thread back through the faceted bead as before, and pull the thread tight, drawing the drops up to the bead and making a cluster.

Continue beading. Your loose spaced clusters are in the foreground.

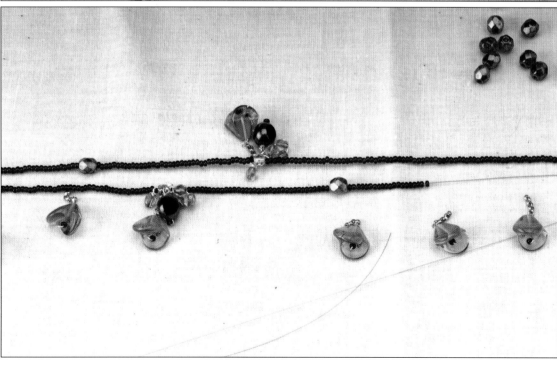

Wrap the thread around the opposite pin and begin your third strand.

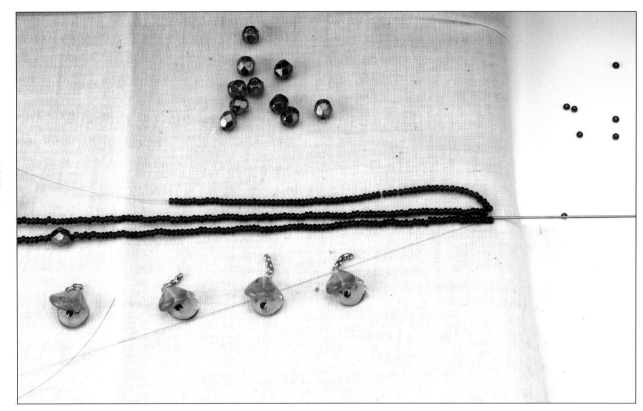

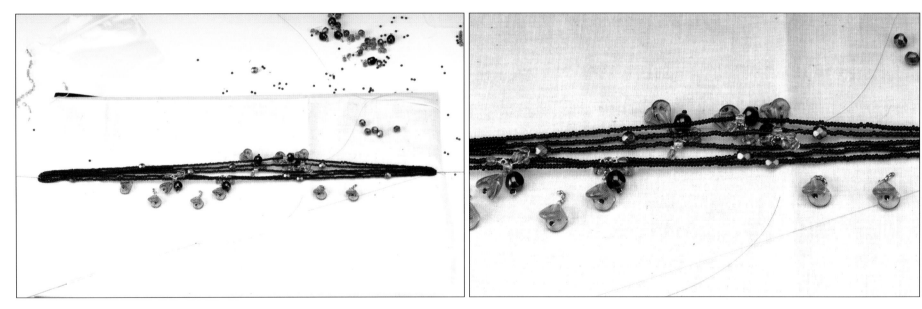

We are half-way done. Five strands are complete.

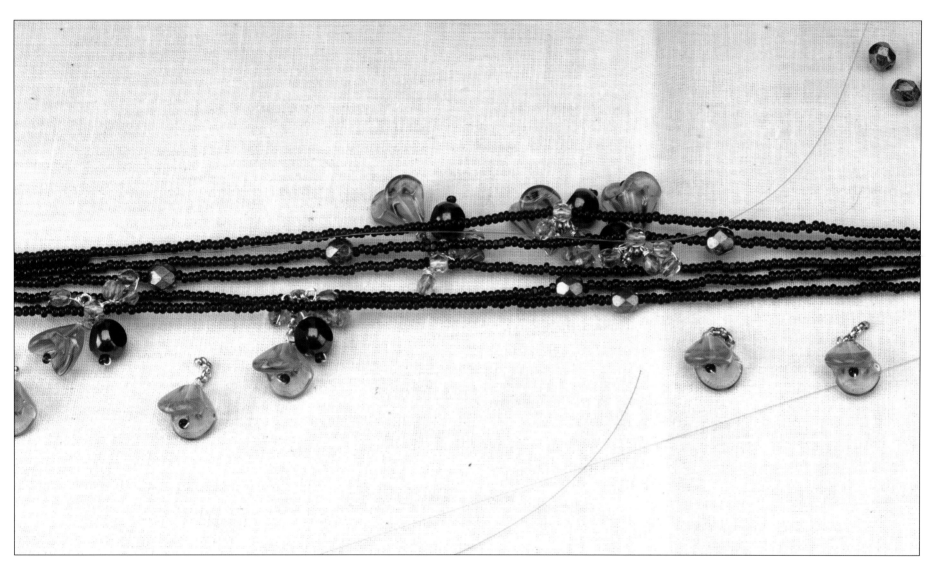

All the drops are strung for the sixth strand.

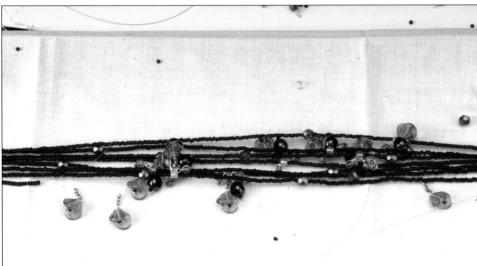

Eight strands are in place.

It's time to place the last cluster of drops on the tenth strand.

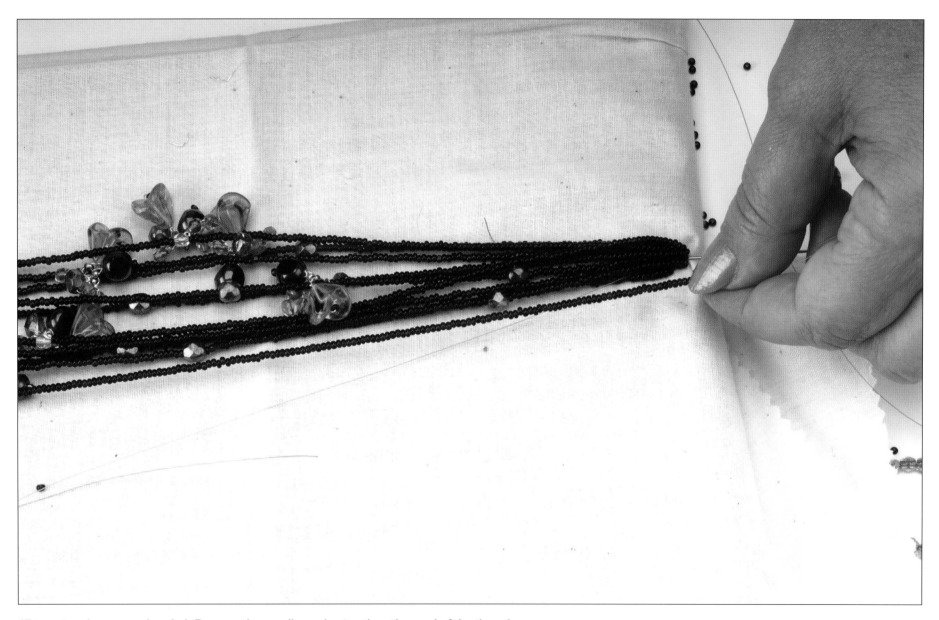

All ten strands are now beaded. Remove the needle anchoring the other end of the thread.

Tie the two ends of the thread tightly at the point where the necklace is anchored with a pin.

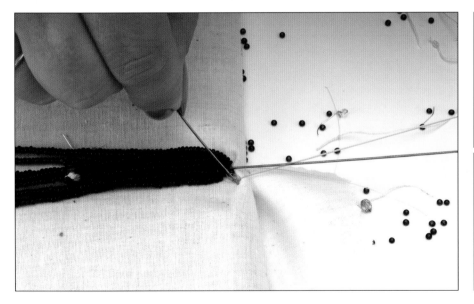

Knot this end again. This is the knot that holds the necklace together.

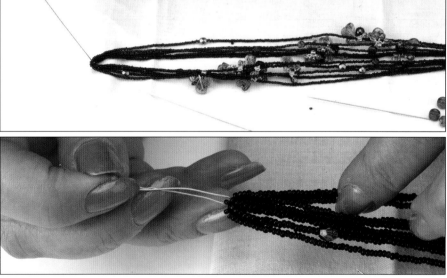

Loosen the pin at one end and slide a 5-inch wire and fold the wire. This wire will hold the necklace together. Repeat on the other side.

Now there is a folded wire at either end and the necklace is loose.

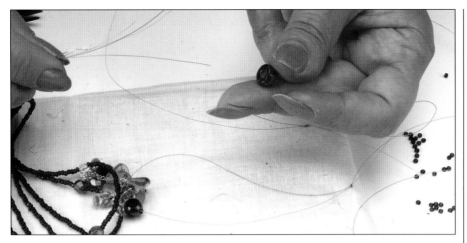

Put a large-hole bead and an 8 mm bead on both ends of the folded 5" wire and the loose threads.

Two beads are placed on the wires and thread ends.

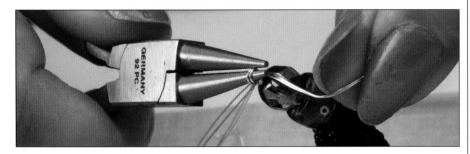

Push the beads down tight. Using round-nosed pliers, wrap the wire around the pliers to create a loop.

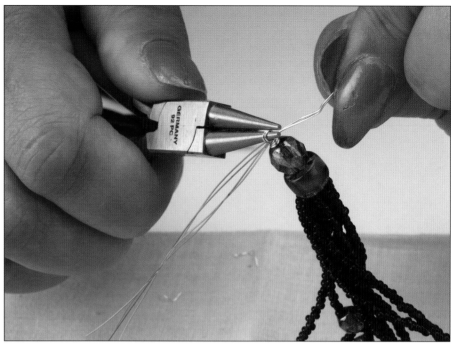

Wrap the end of the wire around the base of the loop to secure the loop tightly and complete it.

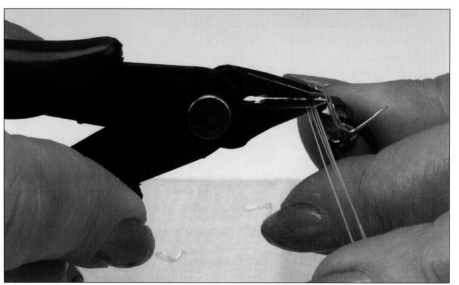

Cut off the excess thread and wire.

The end is complete.

Repeat this process on the other side.

The two ends of the necklace.

Run wire through one of the loops, bend, and make a loop with the pliers.

Add a bead and fold the wire back around the pliers and create a loop as before.

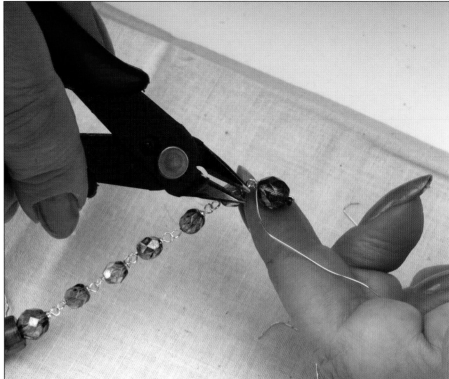

Cut away the excess wire. Repeat this process five times to create a beaded chain as the fastener for this necklace.

Add a larger bead to the end of the bead chain, using the same loop technique to fasten the bead into place.

Use a jump ring to connect the S-shaped hook to the other end of the necklace, and you are finished.

Kits are available for the jewelry in this book.

The completed ten-strand necklace.

This is the kit that may be ordered for the ten-strand necklace.

# Beaded Coil Choker

A beaded coil choker is made using memory wire and 6 lb. fine fishing line.

The bead color palette for a choker necklace, using 6 lb fishing line string and memory wire.

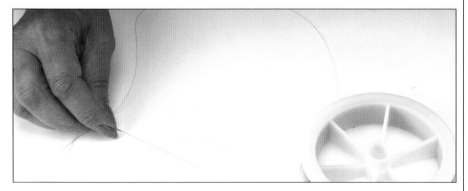

For this project, thread your 6 lb monofilament (fishing line) string onto the needle, but do not cut the thread until the necklace is complete.

Start by stringing thirty-five small 4 mm faceted beads.

Now we're going to start repeating a pattern: five seed beads followed by one round bead, five more seed beads and one faceted 4 mm bead. Repeat this pattern until you have used forty-five round beads in all. If you make a mistake in the pattern repeat, you need to correct it now or the necklace cannot be finished.

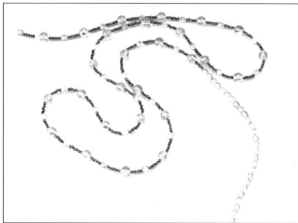

Keep on stringing and be sure to maintain the pattern.

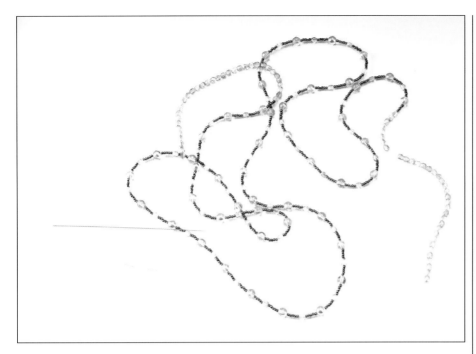

The beads are now all in place, including thirty-five identical crystal beads at either end.

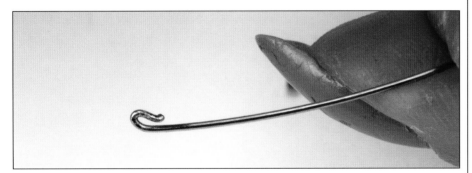

With heavy pliers, fold one end of the memory wire.

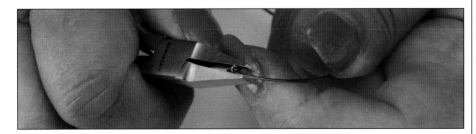

Make the fold as tight, flat, and small as you can.

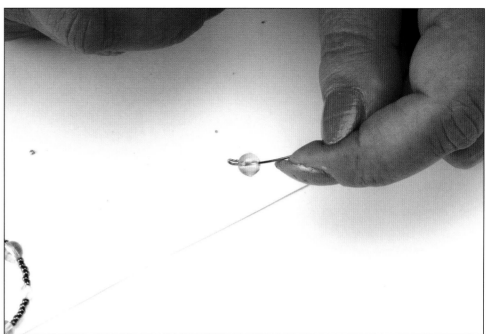

Place one pink bead on the memory wire.

Remove the needle. Do not cut the string from the spool.

Put the threaded beads onto the memory wire, starting with the 35 faceted beads. Do not remove or cut the string.

When you reach the bead pattern, start putting only the faceted beads on the memory wire.

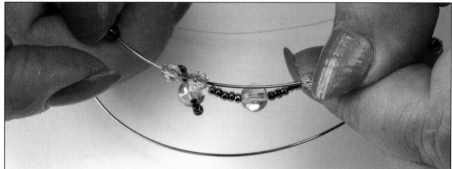

Keep the string tight as you go. It's easy to tighten now, but impossible when all the beads are on the memory wire.

The beads are now on the memory wire.

Add a pink bead to finish off the necklace and make sure all the beads are tight.

Now you can cut the thread.

Trim the exposed end of the memory wire. Using strong pliers, fold over the wire's end very close to the last bead and make it as short, tight, and small as you can.

We want this end loop to be tight enough so that a bead with a large hole will fit over it.

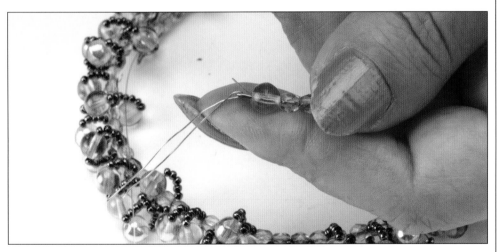

Cut the remaining loose thread. Put a 5-inch wire through the newly created loop at the end of the memory wire and fold in half.

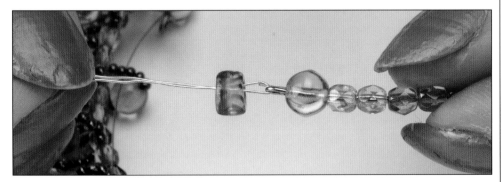

Slide a bead with a large hole over the two ends of the folded wire and push it close to the pink bead.

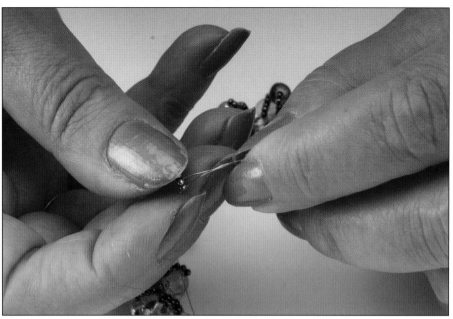

Now slide a medium bead onto the wires close to the bead with the large hole.

The big holed bead covers the loop at the end of the wire and the small bead covers the connection between the loop and the wires.

Make a loop with the wires.

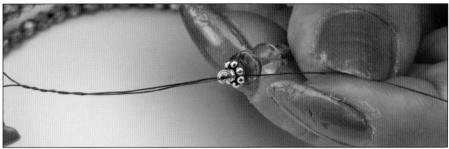

Using a little wire and a bead, add a final finishing bead to the loop, using the same techniques as before.

Trim off the excess wire and the loop is complete. Repeat this process on the other side of the necklace.

The completed necklace.

# Seed Bead Loop Earrings

A pair of seed bead loop earrings is made next.

For the loop earring, begin by stringing two strands of seed beads with some other beads that are exactly the same in bead sequence and length. Each string shown here is 13" long.

Leave the strand a little loose.

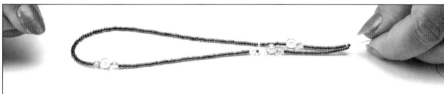

Fold the strung beads in half.

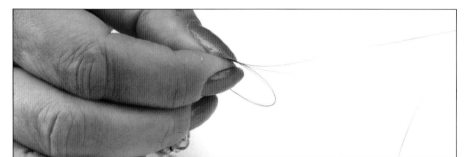

Tie the loose ends together.

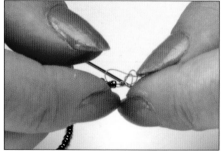
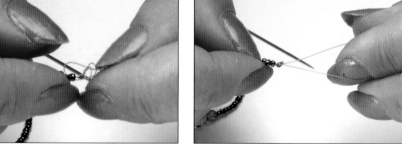

Tie the knot again and make sure the new knot is right on top of the old knot to make it very strong and clean.

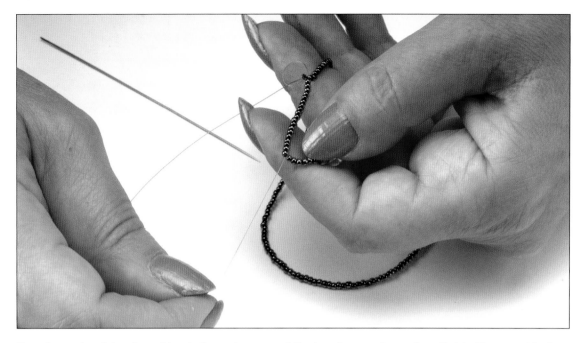

Run the ends of the thread back through some of the beads to make a clean finish. Repeat with the second thread on the other side.

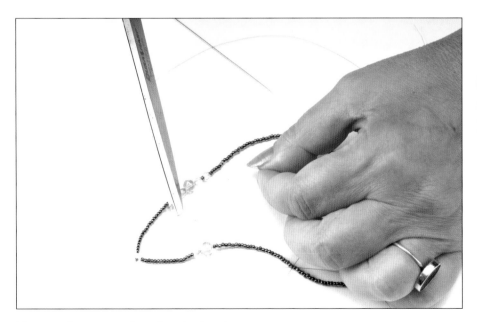

Now cut the excess thread on both sides.

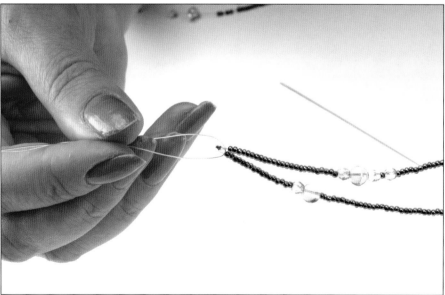

Take a wire and fold it in half.

Now loop the beaded strand over the folded wire loosely…

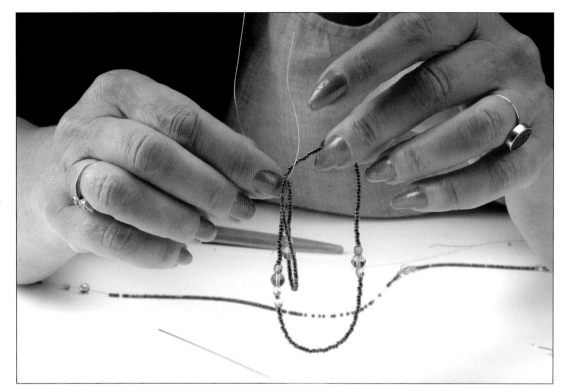

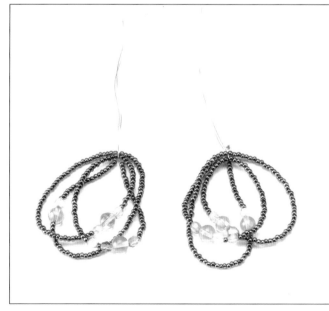

… several times to create three loops. Repeat these steps for the second earring.

The two earrings should look the same.

Slide a little bead cap over the two wire ends to hold the earring together.

Make a loop with the wire and tightly wrap the wire beneath the loop and above the bead cap to hold it in place.

Cut off the excess wire.

The earring loop is complete and bead cap secure. Repeat with the other earring.

Connect the earring to the earwire.

The completed earrings.

# Ani Afshar's Beaded Fantasies Gallery

Enjoy studying these variations that Ani Afshar has made of the designs described in this book. You will be inspired to branch out by creating your own styles. The basic instructions are the same, but your choices of colors, sizes, and materials can be varied.

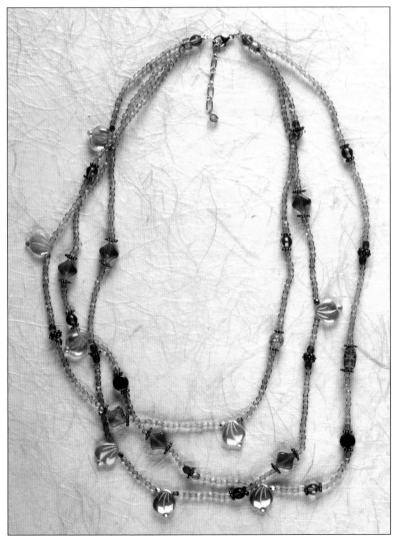

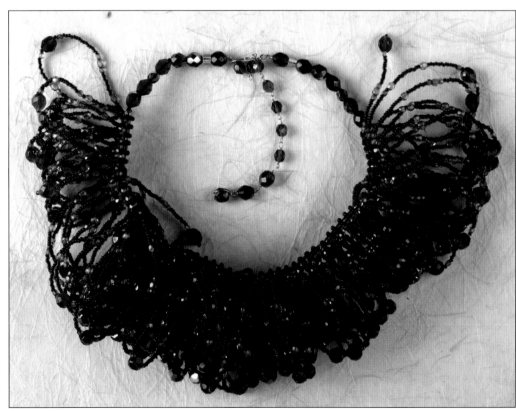

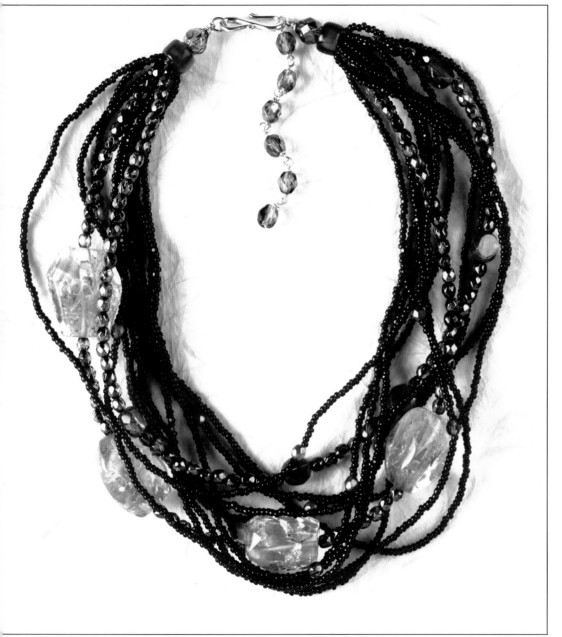

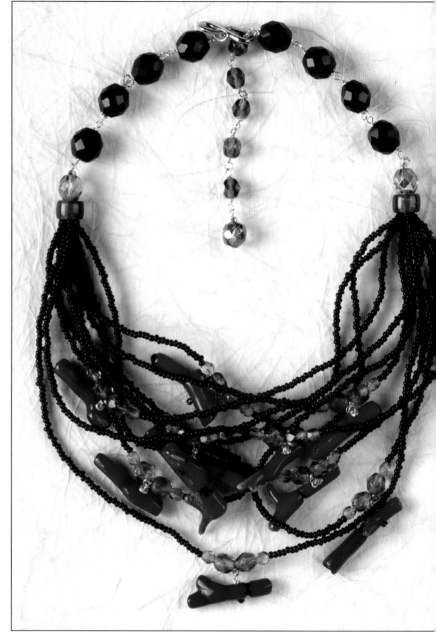

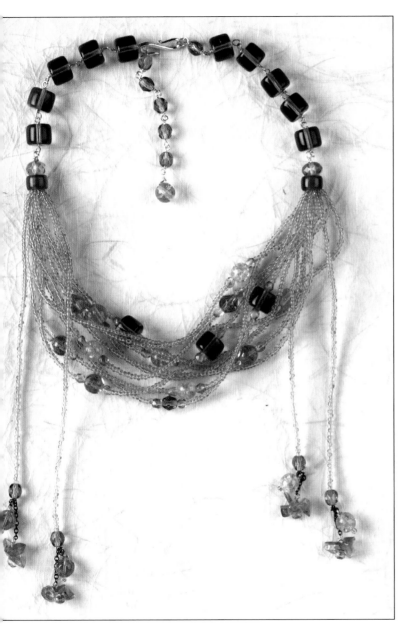

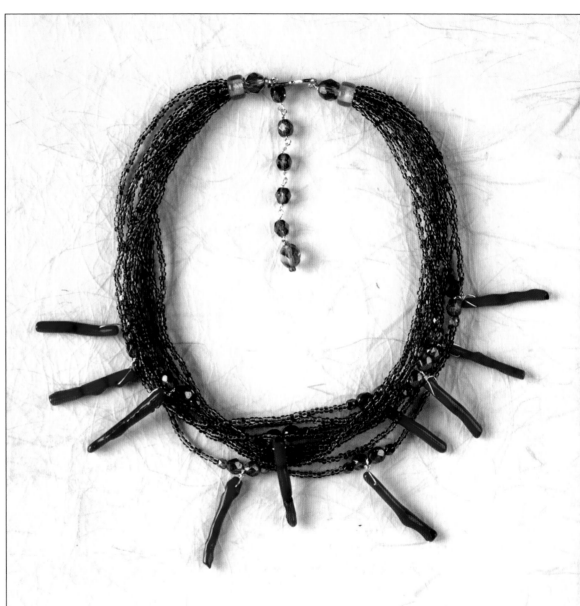

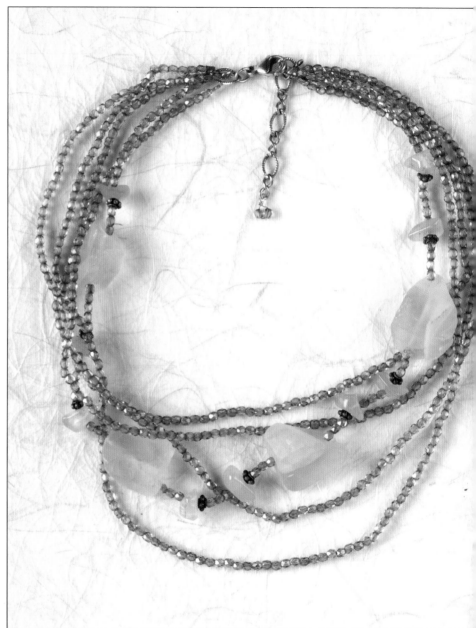

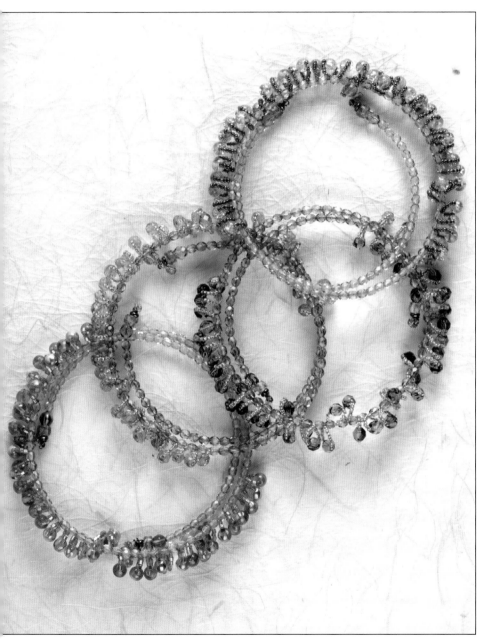